A DAY IN THE LIFE OF AN
FBI Agent-in-Training

by Carter Smith
Photography by Franz Jantzen

Troll Associates

Library of Congress Cataloging-in-Publication Data

Smith, Carter, (date)
   A day in the life of an FBI agent-in-training / by Carter Smith;
photography by Franz Jantzen.
      p.   cm.
   Summary: Portrays the daily training regimen of an FBI agent-
recruit as he learns the skills and techniques of law enforcement.
   ISBN 0-8167-2210-2 (lib. bdg.)   ISBN 0-8167-2211-0 (pbk.)
   1. United States. Federal Bureau of Investigation—Officials and
employees—Training of—Juvenile literature.   2. Police training—
United States—Juvenile literature.   [1. United States. Federal
Bureau of Investigation—Vocational guidance.   2. Police—Vocational
guidance.   3. Vocational guidance.]   I. Jantzen, Franz, ill.
II. Title.
HV8144.F43S65   1991
363.2 '023 '73—dc20   90-11150

The author and publisher would like to thank Supervisory Special Agents Steven
P. Markardt and Ray Jones, and the FBI Academy for their generous assistance
and cooperation.

Photo credits: pp. 4 (top), 13 (bottom)—Federal Bureau of Investigation Academy.

Alex Wong is an agent-in-training at the Federal Bureau of Investigation Academy. It is the most modern law enforcement training facility in the world. Each year the FBI Academy graduates hundreds of young men and women into the most elite law enforcement organization in the United States. Alex Wong is in the seventh week of a rigorous fourteen-week training program.

The FBI Academy is located on a 385-acre campus at Quantico, Virginia, 40 miles south of Washington, D.C. Alex is part of a class of forty trainees, all between the ages of 23 and 35. Each trainee has passed a selection process that includes mental, physical, and psychological tests. At seven in the morning Alex arrives at the library to study for an arrest procedures test.

Alex must be familiar with the law—especially the laws that affect the procedures for making arrests. An arresting agent must inform a suspected criminal of his right to have a lawyer present before making any statements about his guilt or innocence.

During the fourteen weeks of the academy program, Alex and his classmates must achieve scores of 85 percent or better on exams in several academic categories in addition to legal procedures. The curriculum includes learning about human behavior, interviewing techniques, FBI field office administration, fingerprinting and laboratory clue analysis, types of crimes, and communications.

In the academy's sixteen ultramodern classrooms, the instructor can ask questions in front of the class or project them onto a screen. A key skill that FBI agents-in-training must acquire is the use of personal computers for data retrieval and report writing.

Most of the FBI's investigative work does not require the use of firearms, but in some cases agents do need to use guns when making arrests. Therefore academy students spend many hours practice-firing on the firearms ranges. Alex signs out a revolver from the academy's gun vault for a practice session on the range.

Hundreds of thousands of rounds of live ammunition are fired on academy ranges each year. Safety is rigidly enforced at all times by academy instructors at the firing line, who are under the watchful eye of the Principal Firearms Instructor in the range control tower. Alex takes practice shots with an automatic rifle.

The basic weapon carried by all FBI Special Agents on duty is the Smith and Wesson .357 magnum revolver. By their seventh week in the program, all academy trainees must demonstrate great skill with the weapon in a variety of positions, from 5 to 50 yards. An instructor counsels Alex on shooting procedure.

An instructor examines the targets and comments on each trainee's marksmanship. In addition to firing from a fixed position, trainees are trained in practical "combat" shooting—firing at "pop-up" targets. The required scores for firearms qualification are the same for male and female agents. After range practice all trainees must carefully clean their weapons.

At twelve noon it is time for the lunch break in the strenuous academy program. In the cafeteria Alex and his classmates eat a nourishing meal and drink plenty of liquids since they know that a very active afternoon lies ahead of them.

Physical training and defensive tactics are a very
important part of the training that FBI agents receive at the academy. Gym class begins with stretch-
ing exercises. Trainees learn the correct method
of handcuffing a person who is resisting arrest.
There are also classes in boxing and wrestling.

While competitive sports help build the defensive skills that trainees need—such as confidence, aggressiveness, and balance— trainees must also build up their strength. Calisthenics and light exercises help to tone the muscles and build stamina. Trainees who want a more strenuous exercise routine work out with weights. Men and women trainees compete on equal terms.

Trainees at the academy must pass physical training tests in five events. One is the two-mile run, which must be completed in 16 minutes and 30 seconds for men and 18 minutes and 45 seconds for women. Pull-ups is the only other test that has different requirements for men and women. Alex notes records set by male and female trainees.

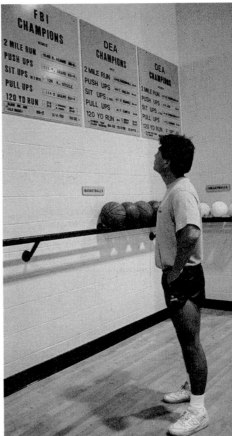

In their law enforcement work, FBI agents can expect to find themselves in many different kinds of locations. Training in the academy's pool builds the trainees' confidence in their ability to operate in the water. An instructor briefs the class before they start their swimming exercise.

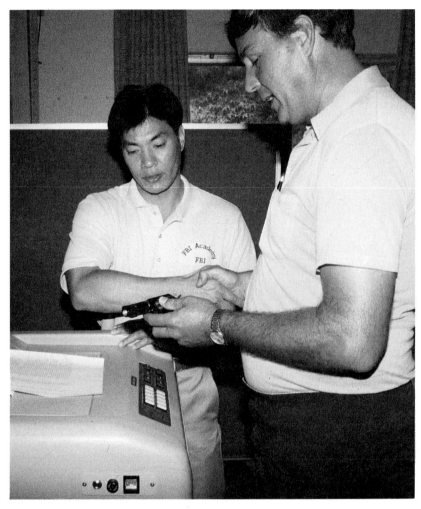

Trainees learn how to use firearms on the firing range, but it is equally important to learn *when* to use a weapon. One training device that forces trainees to make judgment calls is the Firearms Training System. A technician starts the video projector, which presents trainees with different situations in which they must decide whether it is a "shoot" or "no-shoot" situation.

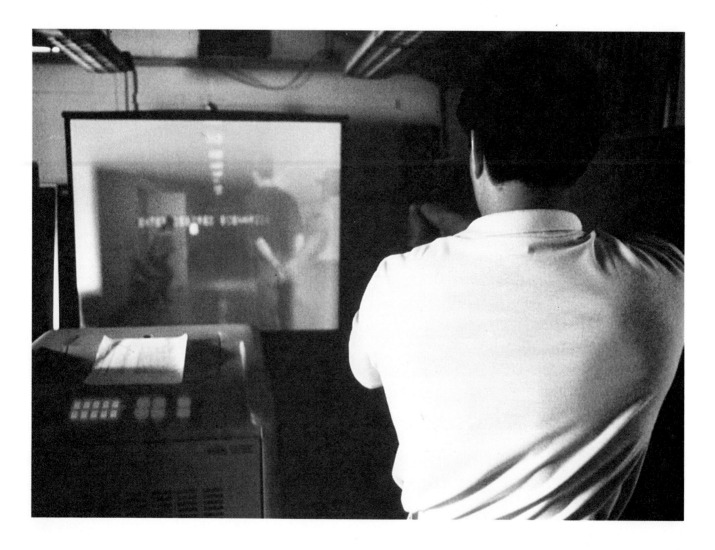

In this exercise, the video shows Alex that he is in a police station accompanying a suspect. On the screen a woman suddenly jumps up from a bench and runs forward. Alex makes an instant judgment not to shoot his laser gun. Since the woman did not have a gun, the system projects "good judgment." If it had been a "shoot" situation, hits and misses would also be scored.

A special training facility called Hogan's Alley is a full-sized model of a small town. It is used to test the trainees' skills in the real work they will undertake after graduation. Like most small towns, Hogan's Alley contains commercial as well as residential buildings. Training exercises in *surveillance* (observing and following), interviewing, gathering evidence, and arrests are conducted here.

Special academy instructors in the Practical Applications Training Unit stage a variety of "mock crimes" that challenge trainees' skills. Professional actors portray criminals, victims, and witnesses. Alex will investigate a kidnapping. Two "criminals" abduct a young woman at gunpoint and force her into a car. Trainees do not see this, but a witness does.

The witness who has observed the kidnapping is a post office employee. She runs out to the sidewalk in time to see the criminals' car leaving the scene. She calls the police and reports the crime. In many kidnapping cases, the police will call the FBI in on the investigation.

The criminals take their victim to a Hogan's Alley rooming house. As soon as the FBI is called into the case, Alex and another agent-in-training go to the post office to conduct a detailed interview with the witness. Unfortunately, she did not get the license plate number of the kidnappers' car.

While Alex and his partner continue to gather more evidence, the mock case continues. A kidnapper telephones the young victim's parents to demand that ransom money be left in a box in a trash bin near the Biograph Theater.

After the money is left in the trash bin, Alex and a partner *stake out* the site to see who arrives to pick up the box. The agents-in-training keep watch from a nearby building so they are out of sight. If the suspects learn that they are being watched, the whole case could be ruined.

After the money is picked up, Alex "dusts" the trash bin for fingerprints while two other agents follow the suspect. Alex will send the prints to the central FBI files center—which contains more than 190 million fingerprint cards—to find a "match-up" for the prints he found.

Once the criminals have the money, they release their victim. By following the kidnapper who picked up the ransom money, the trainees on stake-out have learned the location of the hideout and are prepared to move in as soon as they receive word that the young woman is safe.

As the actor-criminals count their ransom money,
Alex and a heavily armed team of trainees and instructors kick in the door and make the arrest. The
kidnappers are informed of their rights and taken
into custody.

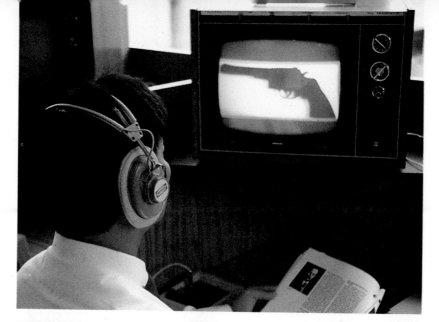

The trainees' next task is to gather and document the evidence needed to gain a conviction in court. Alex does some research on the weapons that were used during the kidnapping, and he consults with laboratory analysts about the blood samples that have been collected.

The kidnapping victim had scratched the face of one of her captors. Some of his blood, which was found under her fingernails, is analyzed in the academy lab. Just as everyone has unique fingerprints, everyone's blood is unique as well. The lab technician confirms that the suspect's blood matches the blood under the victim's fingernails.

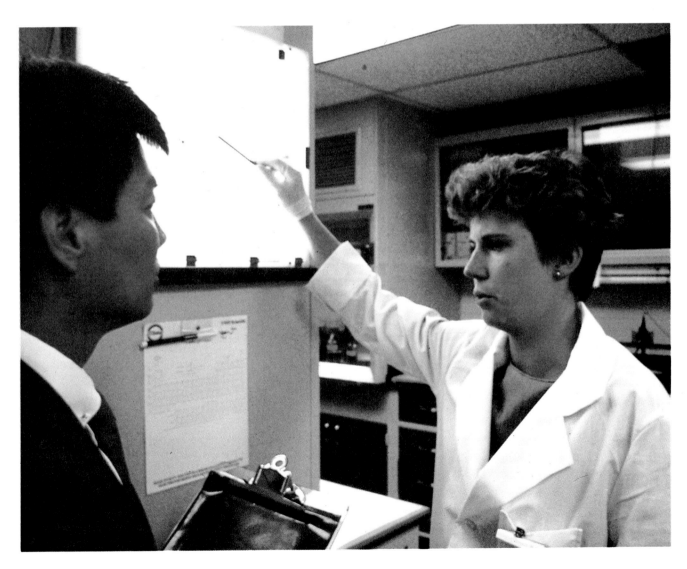

Complicated training cases such as a kidnapping require several days to complete. After a week of building their case, the trainees will appear in a "mock court," where real prosecuting and defending lawyers will question them. Like all agents in FBI field offices, the trainees must testify very carefully. They do not want to lose a case because of a technicality.

Alex heads for the auditorium, where he will attend the graduation of another academy class. He stops with an instructor friend to look at the chart of the "FBI's Ten Most Wanted Fugitives." It is important for agents to be able to remember, recognize, and identify people.

In a typical year 560 highly trained young men and women graduate from the FBI Academy, and they are assigned to the bureau's field offices and Resident Agencies across the country. Alex can feel the glow of pride this class feels in their accomplishments . . . and their glistening gold badges that identify them as FBI Special Agents.